STEP ONE:

Play Tenor Sax

by Sue Terry

Master the basics as you step into the exciting world of playuing the tenor saxophone. A complete and proven method that includes over twenty-five classical and folk tunes to play and enjoy as you learn.

D0613714

PLAYBACK+
Speed • Pitch • Balance • Loop

To access audio visit:
www.halleonard.com/mylibrary

Enter Code
2525-3244-2547-6557

ISBN 978-1-5400-2668-2

Cover photography: Randall Wallace
Project editor: Peter Pickow
Interior design and layout: Len Vogler

Distributed By
HAL•LEONARD®

Visit Hal Leonard Online at
www.halleonard.com

Contact us:
Hal Leonard
7777 West Bluemound Road
Milwaukee, WI 53213
Email: info@halleonard.com

In Europe, contact:
Hal Leonard Europe Limited
42 Wigmore Street
Marylebone, London, W1U 2RN
Email: info@halleonardeurope.com

In Australia, contact:
Hal Leonard Australia Pty. Ltd.
4 Lentara Court
Cheltenham, Victoria, 3192 Australia
Email: info@halleonard.com.au

Contents

Introduction

So you've dreamed of playing the saxophone, but are a little afraid of getting started. Well, with a little study and practice, you can do it. This introductory saxophone method is easy and fun, and gives you all the skills you need to continue learning hundreds of songs on your own, or with a teacher.

Although the saxophone is made of brass, it is a member of the woodwind family and uses a reed to obtain its sound. It is one of the few instruments to be named after its inventor: Belgian instrument maker Adolphe Sax took out a patent on his invention in 1846, although it is thought that the instrument may have existed as early as 1841. Sax envisioned his new instrument becoming part of the orchestral wind section, but it was not to be. Instead, the saxophone was first used by military bands, for its ability to combine the power of a brass instrument with the speed and facility of a woodwind. Little could Sax know that the saxophone was destined to become one of the definitive instruments of the next century. In addition to its extensive use in jazz and pop music, composers such as Debussy, Ravel, Richard Strauss, Bartók, and Hindemith all wrote for it. Today, the saxophone is one of the most popular instruments in the world.

Whether you intend to be a professional saxophonist, or simply wish to play for your community, family, and friends—this book is for you. So, get ready to learn the basics of saxophone as you play some of the world's most popular melodies.

Basics of Music Notation

Here are some basics of music notation:

whole note	𝅝	whole rest	𝄻	=	4 beats
half note	𝅗𝅥	half rest	𝄼	=	2 beats
quarter note	♩	quarter rest	𝄽	=	1 beat
eighth note	♪	eighth rest	𝄾	=	½ beat
sixteenth note	𝅘𝅥𝅯	sixteenth rest	𝄿	=	¼ beat

A whole note is equivalent to 2 half notes, 4 quarter notes, 8 eighth notes, *etc.*

1 whole note = 2 half notes = 4 quarter notes =

8 eighth notes = 16 sixteenth notes

The rhythm is different yet the time taken up is the same.

A dot next to the note (♩.) indicates that one-half of that note's value is to be added to the duration of that note.

For example:

𝅗𝅥. = 𝅗𝅥 + ♩

♩. = ♩ + ♪

♪. = ♪ + 𝅘𝅥𝅯

The same principle applies to rests.

𝄼. = 𝄼 + 𝄽

𝄽. = 𝄽 + 𝄾

𝄾. = 𝄾 + 𝄿

Other basics:

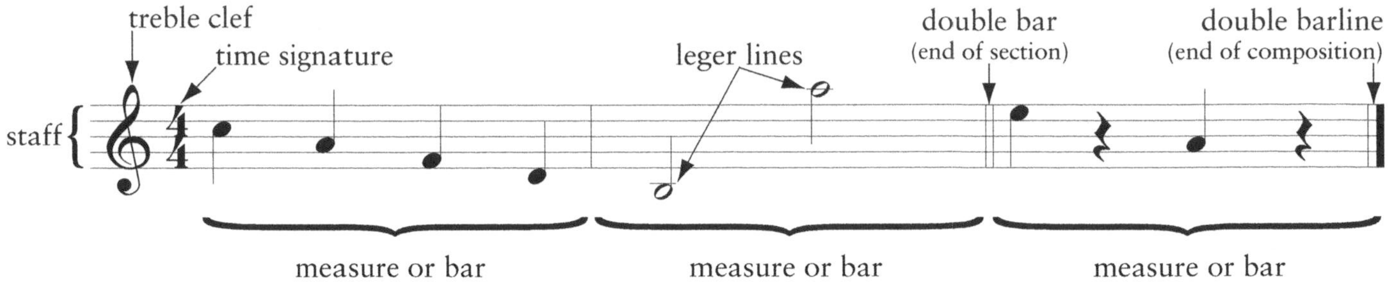

Staff: the five lines and four spaces on which the musical language of notes and symbols are arranged.

Treble clef: Also called the *G clef,* provides a frame of reference for notes placed on the lines and spaces of the staff:

The spaces are

The lines are

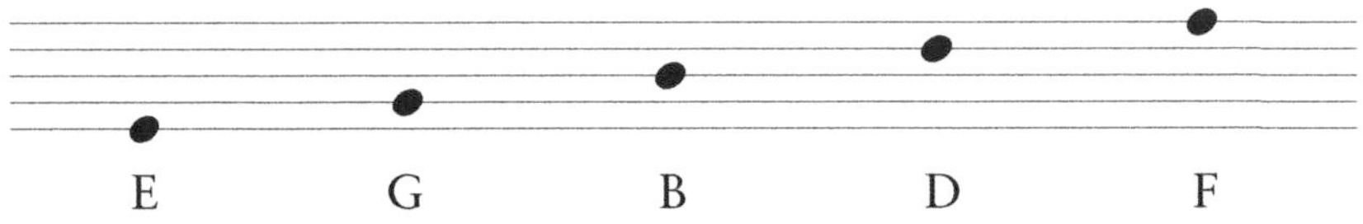

Leger lines: The additional lines used to extend the staff.

Time signature: This symbol indicates two important facts about the overall rhythm of the piece. The top number indicates the number of beats per measure and the bottom number indicates which type of note gets the beat.

Barline: The vertical lines that divide the music on the staff into sections called *measures* or *bars.*

Double barlines: Two thin lines indicate the end of a musical section. One thin line and one thick line indicate the end of the composition.

Accidentals: Symbols used to alter a pitch; a flat (♭) lowers the pitch one half-step, a sharp (♯) raises the pitch one half-step, and a natural (♮) returns the pitch to its unaltered state.

Throughout the book there will be more development and explanation of these and other musical symbols and terms.

Saxophone Basics

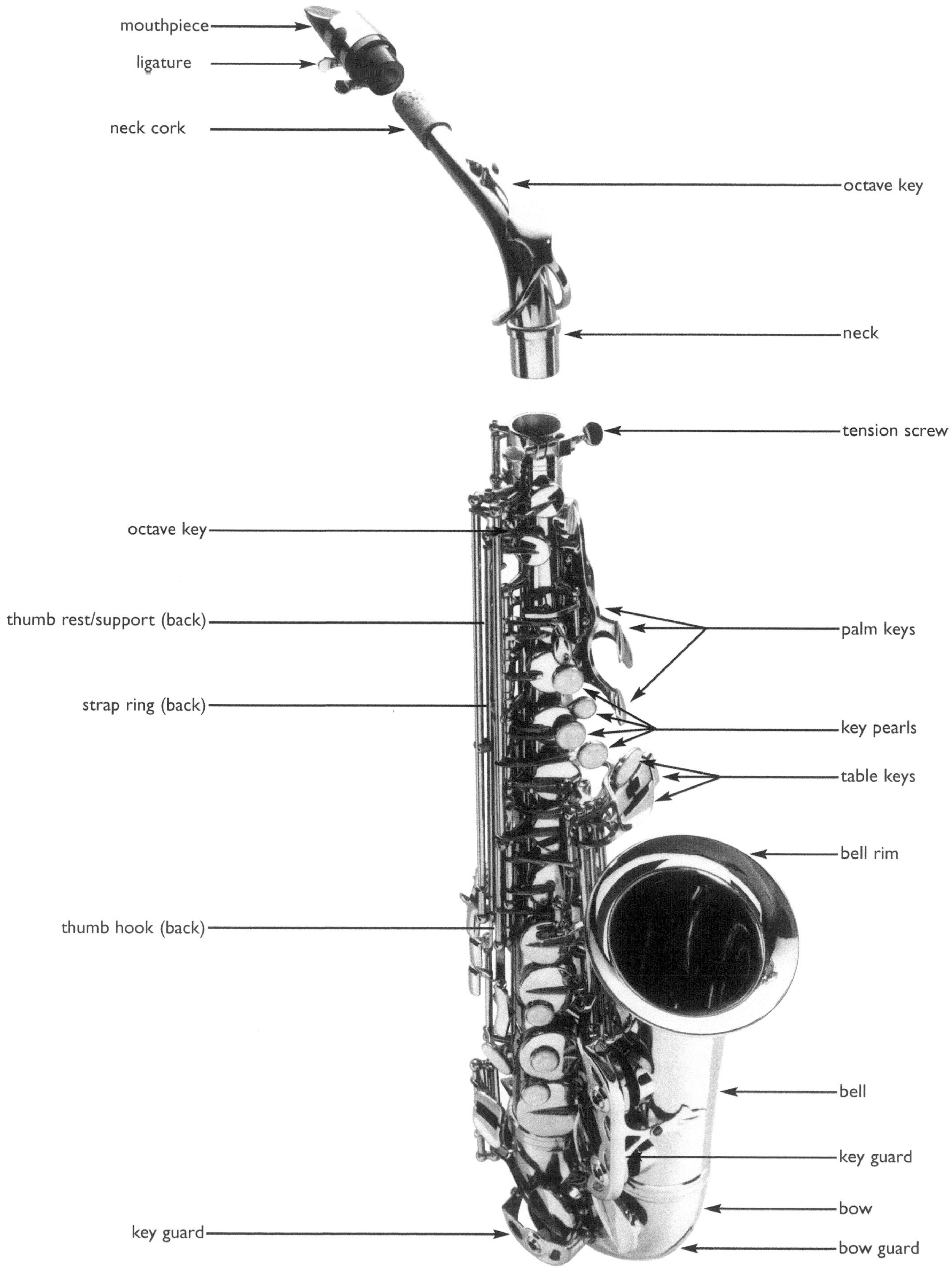

Parts of the Saxophone

Reed (start with a #2, or "Soft"—buy a box of 10)
Ligature (holds reed onto mouthpiece)
Mouthpiece
(Mouthpiece cap—protects reed and mouthpiece)
Neck
(End cap—protects octave key while in case)
Body
Bell
(Neckstrap or harness—supports the instrument)

Accessories

Reedguard
Swabs (One for mouthpiece and neck, one for body)
Cork grease (for neck cork)

Reeds

Reeds should be soaked in warm water for a few minutes before using. If no water is available, a reed can be moistened in your mouth. Extra reeds should be placed in a special holder called a *reedguard.*

Tuning

The saxophone is tuned by twisting (not pushing or pulling) the mouthpiece forward or backward on the neck cork. "Pushing in" makes the horn sharper (higher in pitch) and "pulling out" makes it flatter. The tuning process becomes important when playing with other musicians, or when playing along with the CD for this book!

Saxophone Range

All saxophones have a range of low B♭ to high F or F♯. Higher notes can be played by using special fingerings.

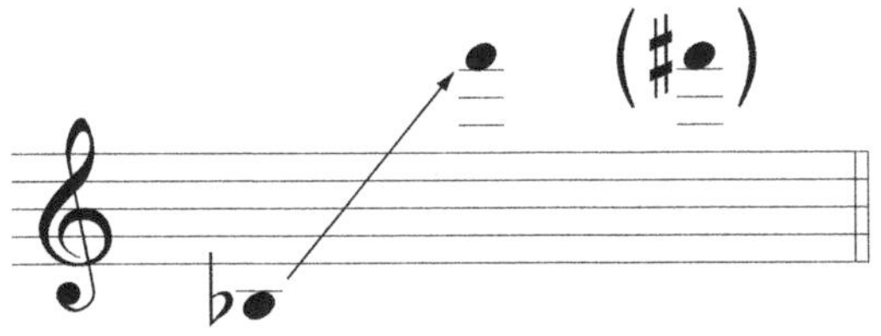

A Note on Transposition

Soprano and tenor saxophones are pitched in B♭, which means that your C is a B♭ on the piano. Alto and baritone saxophones are pitched in E♭, which means that your C is an E♭ on the piano. Besides the piano, other C (nontransposing) instruments include flute, recorder, guitar, and most string family instruments.

Putting It All Together

Let's try making some sounds using only the mouthpiece and neck sections of the horn. First, slip the ligature onto the mouthpiece. *Note: Most ligatures should be placed so that the screws are on the bottom side of the mouthpiece, against the reed.* Lifting the ligature with your left thumb, slide your moistened reed down between mouthpiece and ligature with your right thumb. *Don't touch the tip of the reed!* The tip of the reed should end up slightly beneath the tip of the mouthpiece, so that you still see a very thin line of mouthpiece. Tighten the screws on the ligature only enough to hold the reed in place.

Next, twist the mouthpiece onto the neck cork. On most horns, it will need to cover at least half of the cork. If it doesn't go on so easily, try some cork grease. If it goes on too easily, wrap a piece of paper around the cork to tighten the seal.

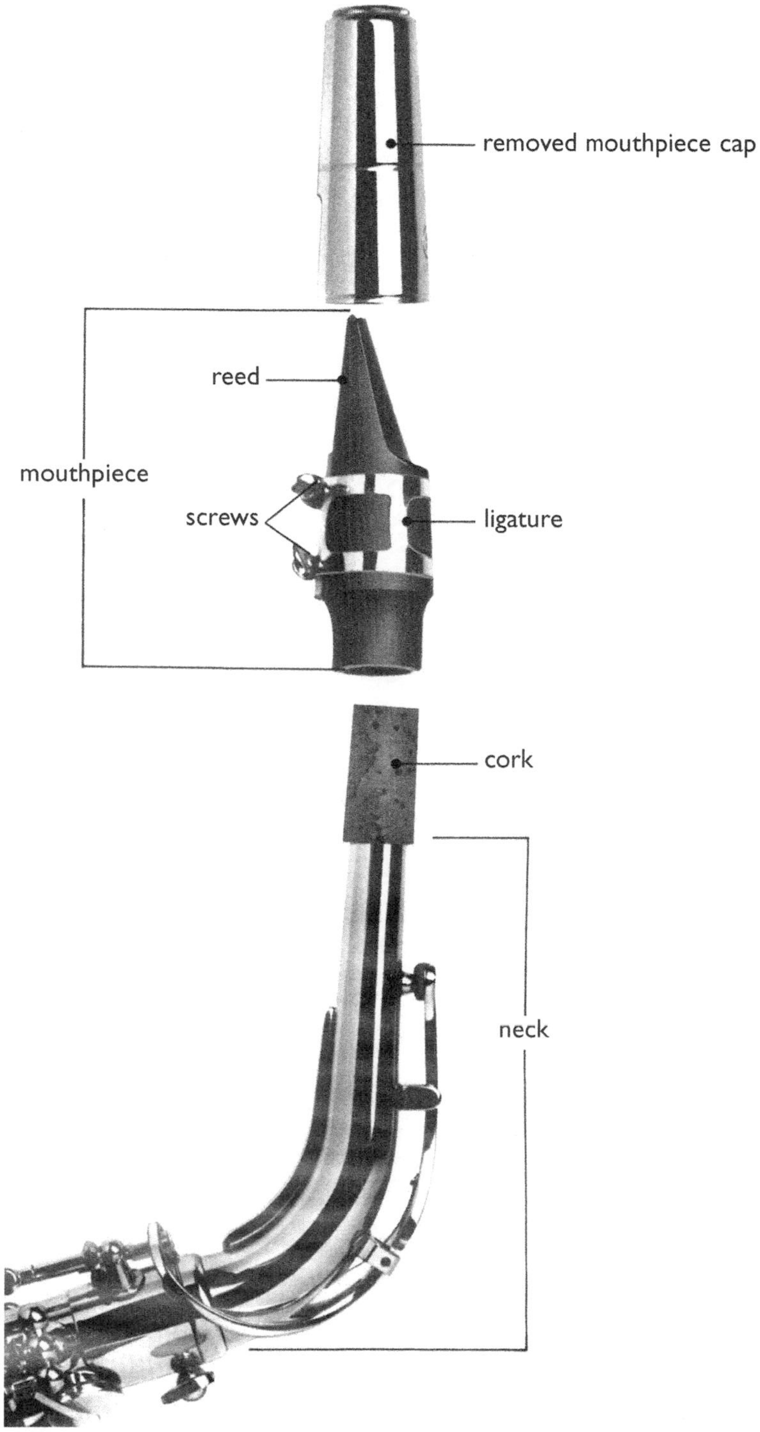

Embouchure

The way we put our mouth on the mouthpiece of any wind instrument has a special name: *embouchure* (ahm-bah-shur).

Here is the usual embouchure for saxophone:

1. Place your bottom lip under the reed, and prevent your bottom teeth from coming in contact with the reed.
2. Top teeth rest on the mouthpiece, one-half inch or so from the tip.
3. Corners of the mouth are kept closed, so no air escapes out the sides.
4. Don't puff out your cheeks!

Take a big breath, and blow a steady stream of air into the mouthpiece/neck combination. Practice holding out this note as long as you can, at a medium volume. Try for a nice, straight tone with no wavering.

Saxophone Position and Fingering

The saxophone is supported by your neckstrap. Slip the hook on the end of the strap throught the small ring on the back of the horn. There are many types of neckstraps available, as well as shoulder slings and harness straps that relieve pressure on your neck. Ask at your local music store, or on the Internet.

Slip the strap over your head, and slip the hook on the end of the strap through the small ring on the back of the horn. Adjust the strap with one hand while holding your horn up, by the bell, with the other hand. When the strap is properly adjusted, the mouthpiece should be able to go directly in your mouth without bending your head down or up.

Put your left hand on top and your right hand on bottom, with the thumbs using their respective thumb rests.

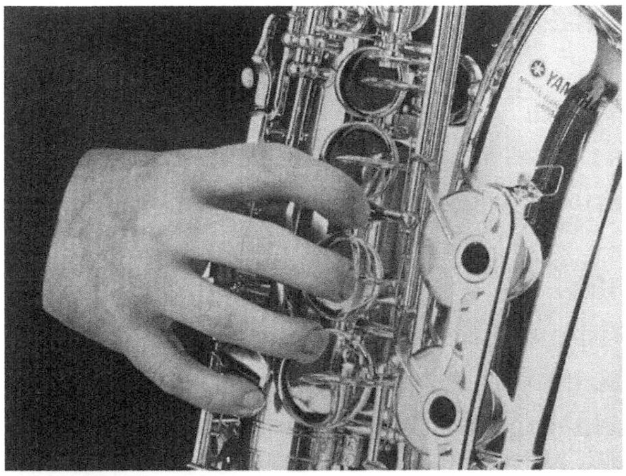

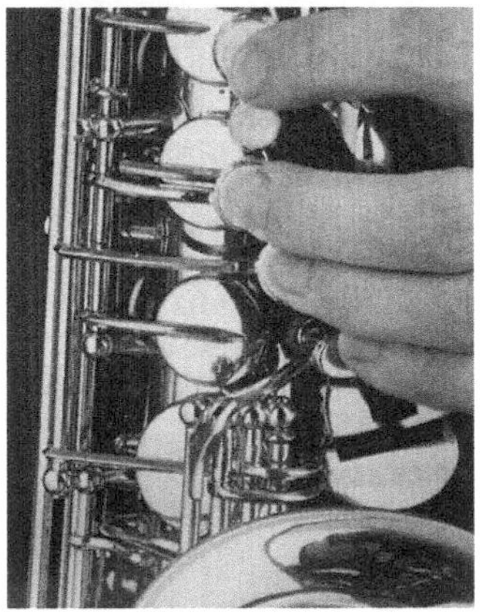

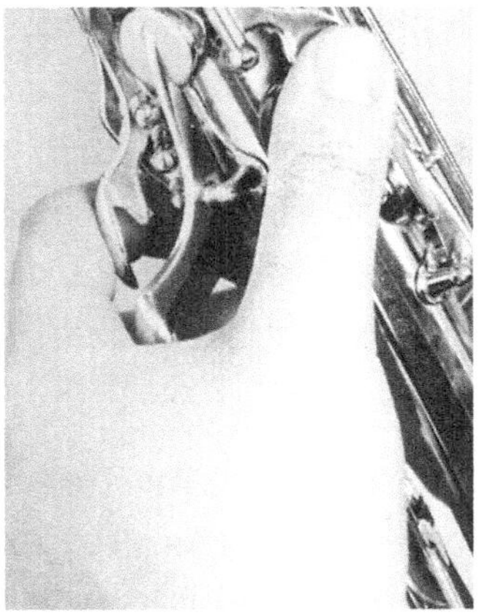

Now that you know how to hold the horn, you'll notice that advertisements with saxophone players often reverse the picture, showing the hands in the wrong position!

The two most dangerous moments in a saxophone's day: taking it out of and putting it back into the case.

Handle your horn with care.

Taking out: Bell first

Putting away: Bell last

Always put the end cap in the top of the body when putting the horn away—it protects your octave key from damage.

Be sure to keep your horn in good working order by having it checked by a qualified repairperson. Adjustments and overhauls can be done via the mail system if you do not live near a good repair shop.

Let's Play

Longtones

Longtones are just that—tones held out for a long time.
They serve to:

- strengthen the embouchure
- improve breath control
- improve tone quality

Let's try some longtones on your first note, middle B.

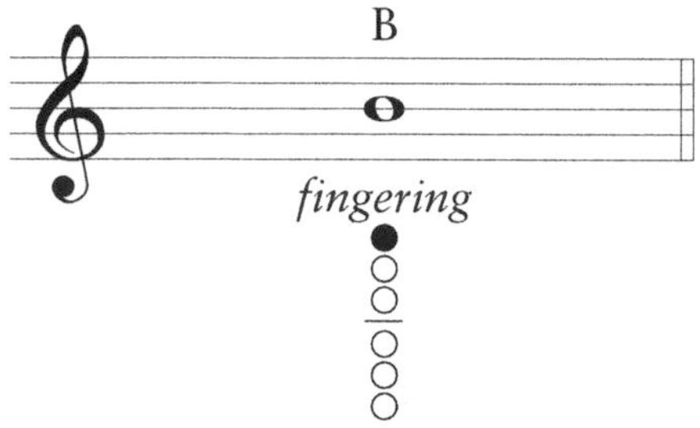

In $\frac{4}{4}$ time there are four beats to a measure.
A *whole note* is worth four beats.

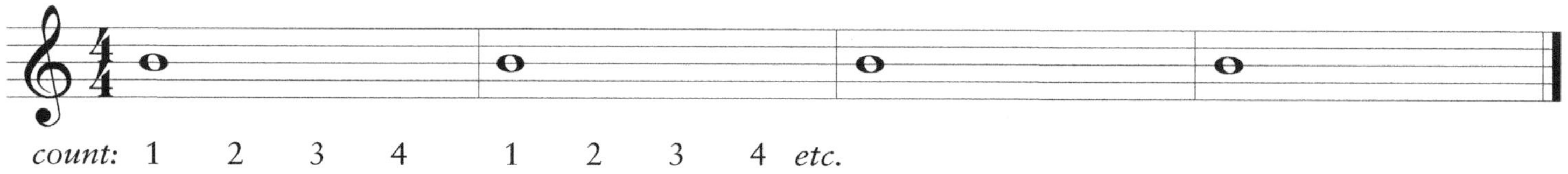

Tonguing

Use your tongue to separate notes, especially consecutive notes on the same pitch. While blowing steadily, touch the tip of your tongue to the tip of the reed—just for an instant. It's like a snake darting its tongue out.

Try this on two more notes, A and G.

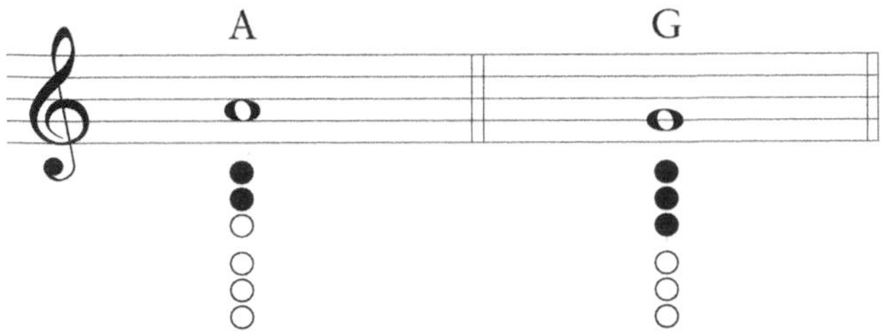

Remember, *half notes* and *half rests* are worth two beats.

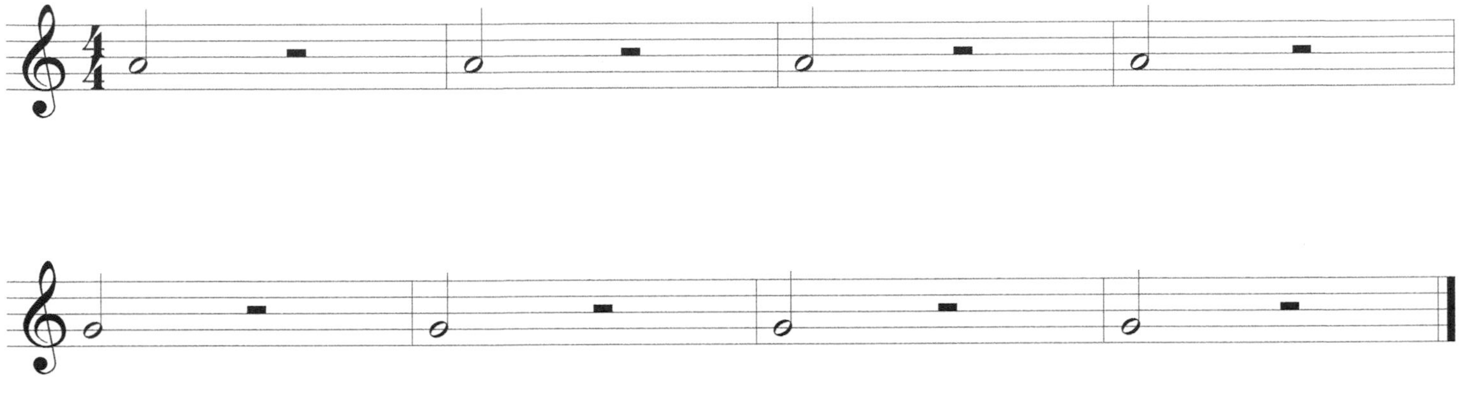

Some practice with B, A, and G.

A *quarter note* is worth one beat.

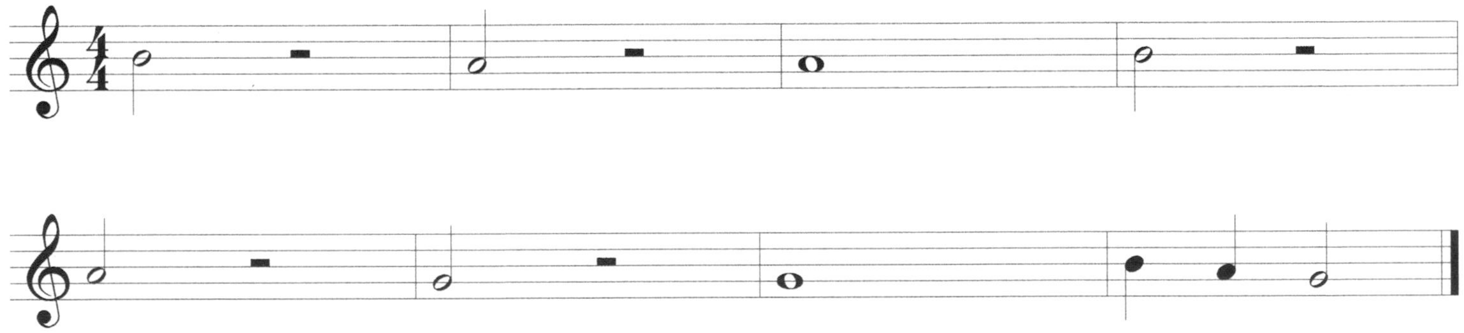

Breathing

Breaths are taken without removing the mouthpiece from the mouth. Simply let your embouchure relax and take a quick breath through the mouth during rests in the music, or between notes.

Easy Songs

Here's your first song; remember to tongue each note.

Au Clair de la Lune

French

Two *eighth notes* are worth one beat.

Hot Cross Buns

English

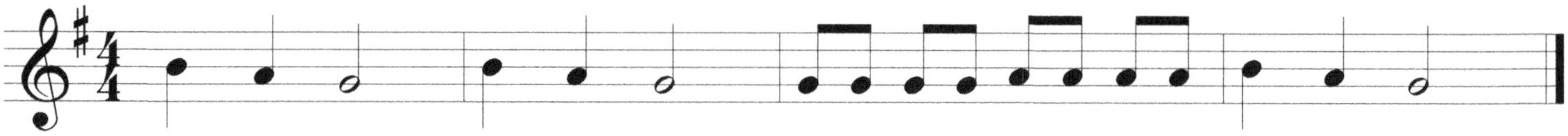

Practice some longtones on all the notes you know so far, plus a new note, C.

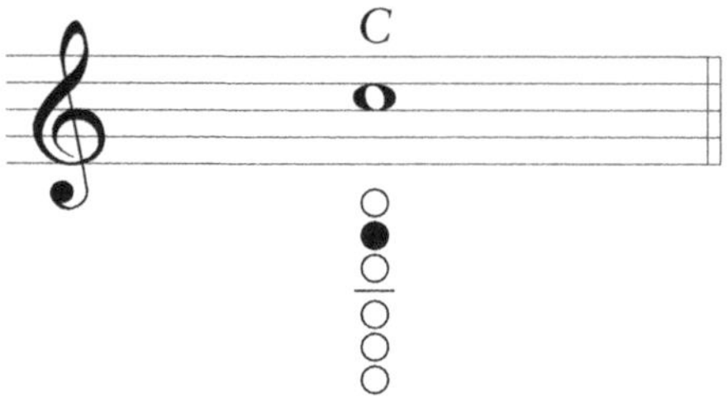

’ = take a breath

When changing fingering from B to C, your fingers must move simultaneously. Try changing from B to C and back again several times without blowing, making your fingers “march” in time to a slow tempo. Once the fingers are used to this, try blowing at the same time.

A *repeat sign* (:‖) tells you to go back to the beginning and play the piece (or section) again.

In $\frac{2}{4}$ time, there are two beats to a measure.

A tie (⌒) connects two notes of the same pitch.

A *dotted half note* gets three beats.

BILE ’EM CABBAGE DOWN

Traditional

Here's a classic melody that uses a new note, F.

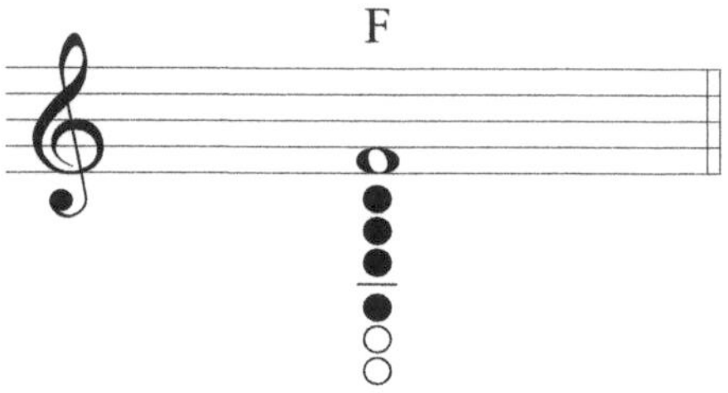

Mary Had a Little Lamb

Traditional

Here's a jazzier version of the same tune. In $\frac{4}{4}$ time, single eighth notes (♪) are worth half of one beat.

Jazzy Mary

New note: B♭.

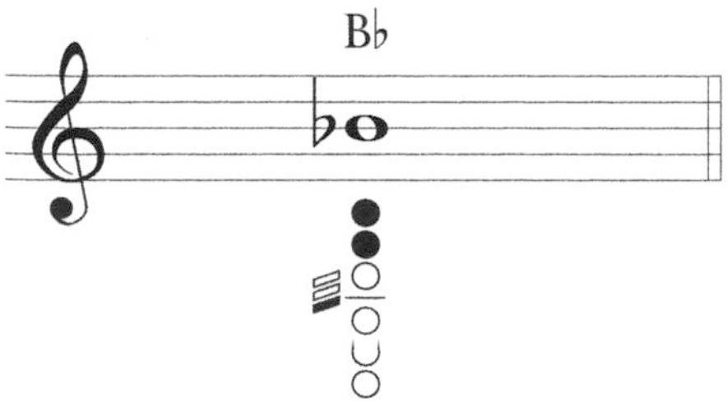

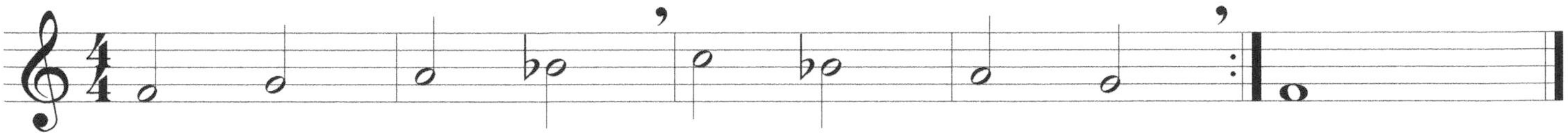

Notice the key signature in this next song. The flat sign (♭) on the line for B indicates that all B's should be played as B♭'s.

When the Saints Go Marchin' In

Traditional

Did you notice that the first measure has only three beats in it? These are called *pickup notes*. Remaining beats from pickup bars are found in the last bar.

Learn both parts of this duet.

Lightly Row

(duet)

Imagine that you straighten out your saxophone (don't try this at home). You'll then realize that it's just a long tube with holes along it. As you add fingers, the pads close off more of the tube, and the air has farther to travel, thus making the notes lower in pitch.

New notes: E, D, C.

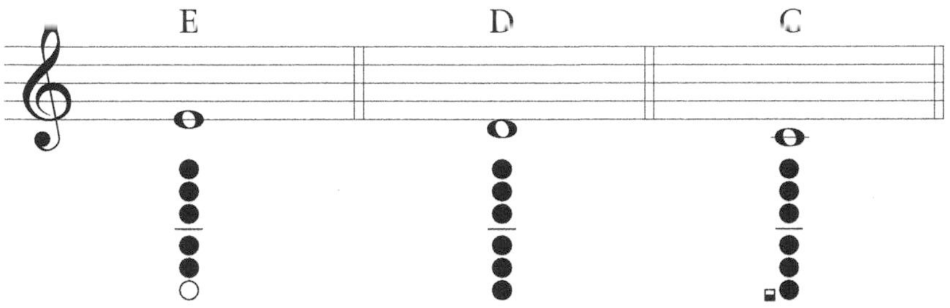

C Major Scale

Low Notes

To get the low notes, take a big breath to fill the entire horn with air. Do not take in more mouthpiece! This will result in an undesirable honking sound. Instead, practice "walking down" to your low notes starting from G. With practice (and a properly adjusted horn) your low notes will begin to pop out more easily.

Getting Down

A *slur* looks like a tie, but it connects notes of differing pitches. Tongue only the first note of a group of slurred notes.

Joy to the World

Traditional

In $\frac{3}{4}$ time, there are three beats to a measure. A dotted quarter note gets one and one-half beats. Take note of the key signature!

The Streets of Laredo

Traditional

The Octave Key

Your left thumb doesn't just sit there on the thumb rest—it controls the *octave key!* Without playing, tilt your thumb (do not lift it from the thumb rest) so it presses the edge of the octave key. When you get accustomed to the feeling of the octave key, try blowing on your low F, then the upper F by adding the octave key. The upper note should sound like the lower note, except one level higher. You will need to adjust your embouchure (remember that word?) as you switch octaves. Remember to tongue each note.

New note: F

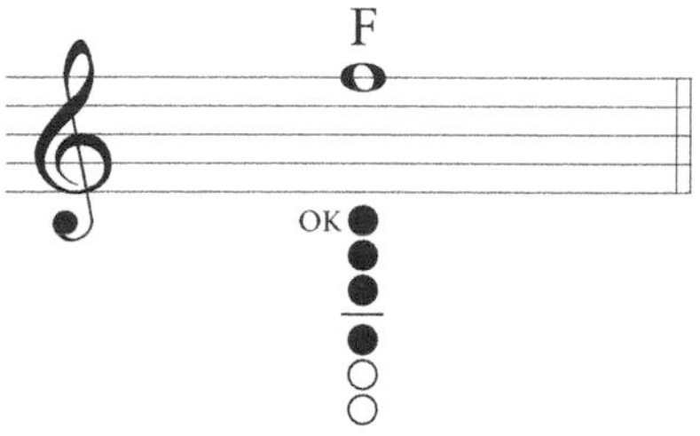

Octave Exercise 1

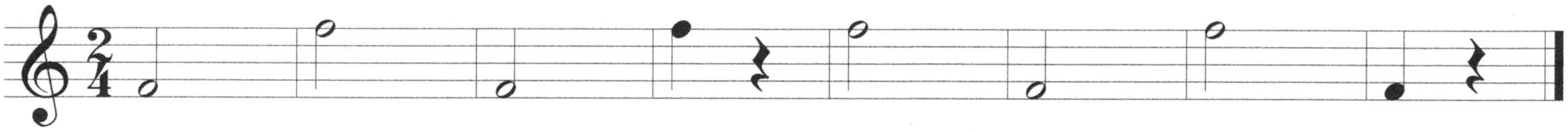

Notice that the fingerings for upper E and D are the same as the lower octave notes, with the addition of the octave key.

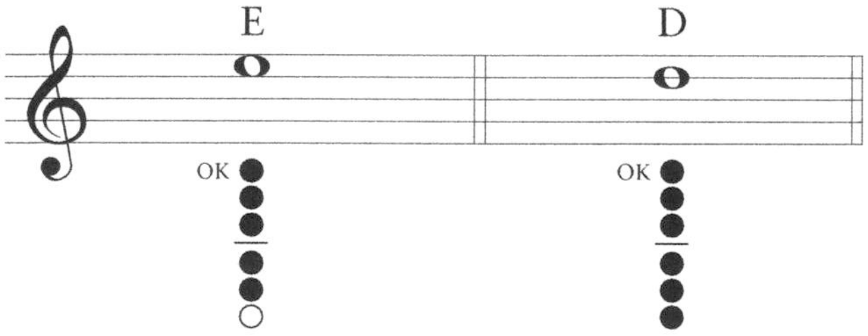

Octave Exercise 2

While playing this F scale, remember to use your octave key on D, E, and F.

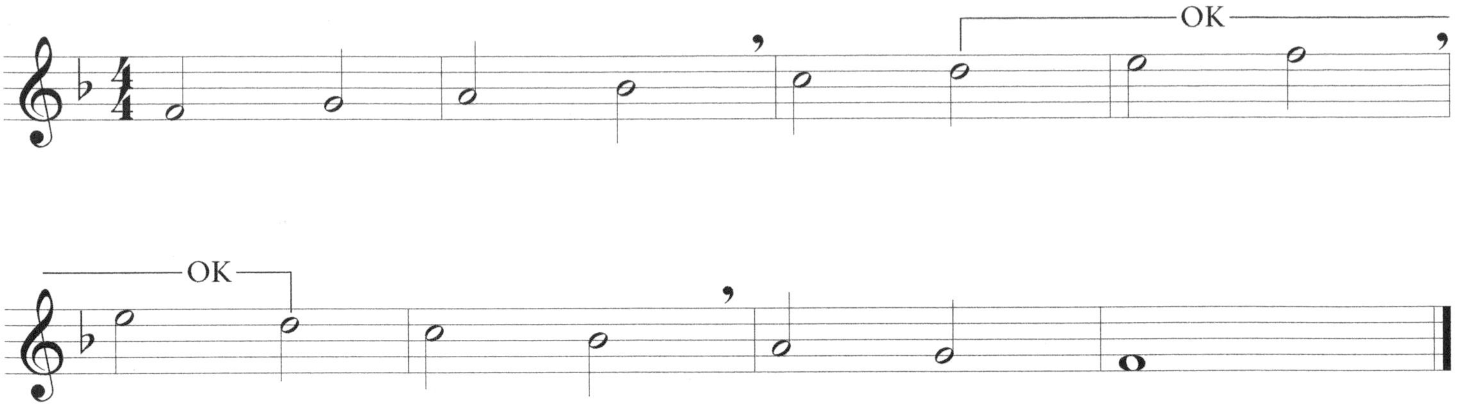

On Top of Old Smokey

Traditional

Frère Jacques is a four-part round with a new part entering every four measures. To play along with the CD, you should come in second; that is, start playing when the first player reaches the number 2. Then play the tune four times through.

Frère Jacques

(ROUND)

French

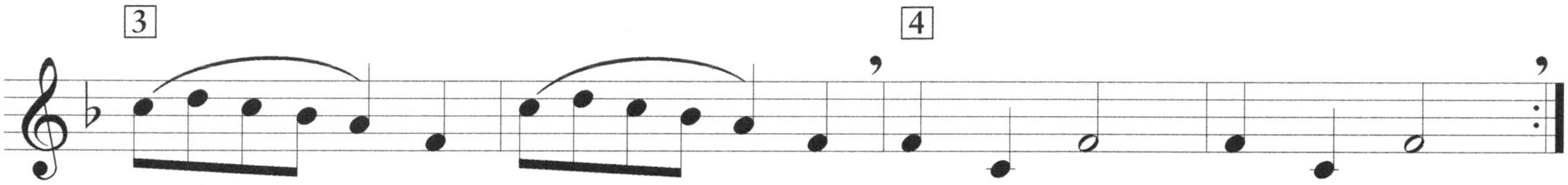

Making a smooth slur on C and D can be tricky. Here's as exercise to help you practice it.

New note: F♯.

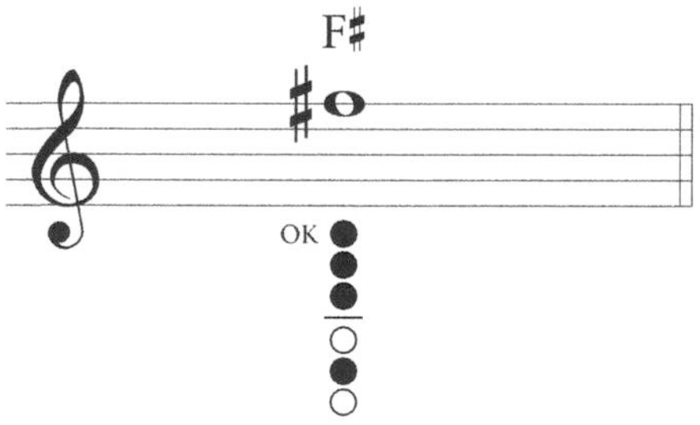

G Major Scale

New note: F♯.

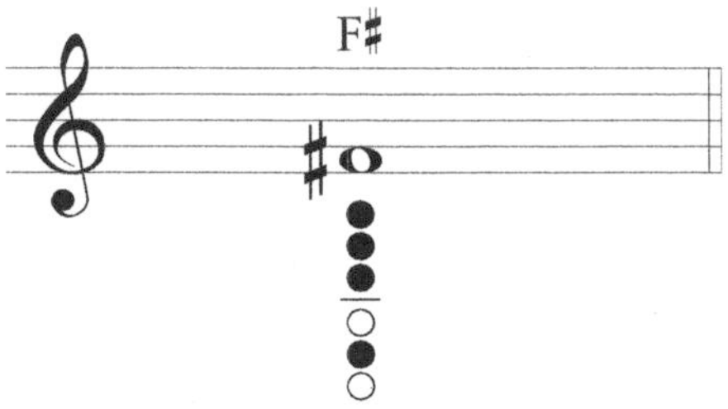

The $\frac{4}{4}$ time signature is often written as 𝄴.

Auld Lang Syne

Scottish

My Country, 'Tis of Thee

English

New note: C♯.

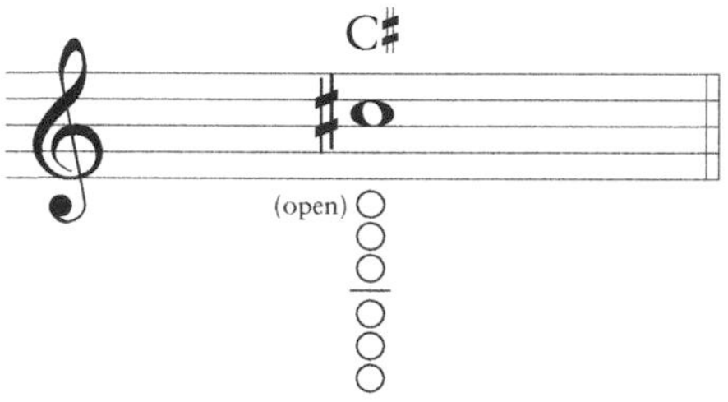

Notes that are outside the key signature are called *accidentals*. Always check your key signature and time signature before starting a tune.

America the Beautiful

American

New notes: E♭, A, and B♭.

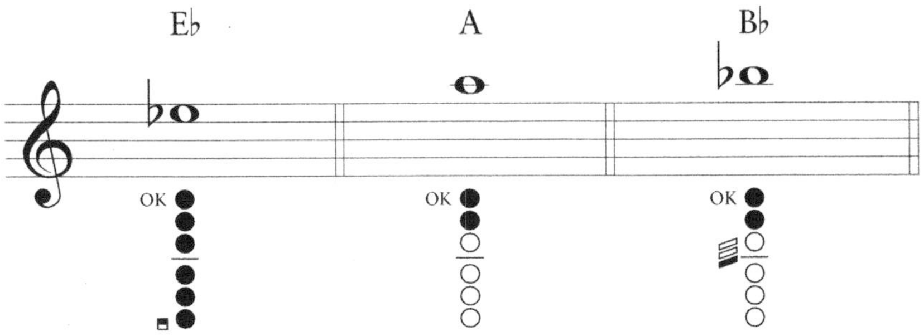

B♭ Major Scale

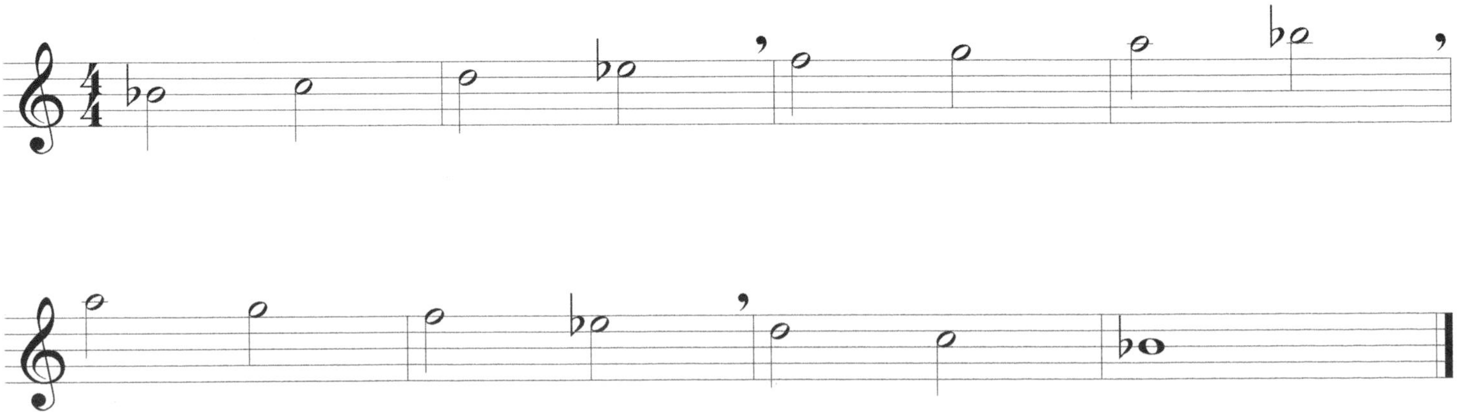

The next song has a key signature of two flats: B♭ and E♭.

The John B. Sails

West Indian

New note: A♭.

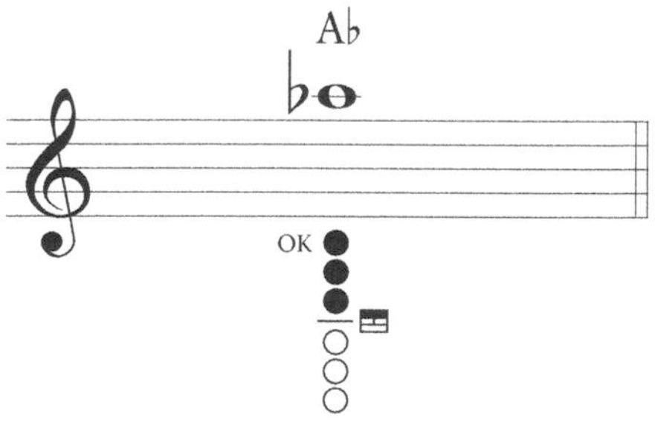

De Colores

Mexican

Dynamics

The use of *dynamics* helps to bring out the feeling of the music.

Dynamic markings

p	=	piano, soft
mp	=	mezzo piano, medium soft
mf	=	mezzo forte, medium loud
f	=	forte, loud
<	=	crescendo, get gradually louder
>	=	diminuendo, get gradually softer
>	=	accent mark, emphasize the note

New note: D♯.

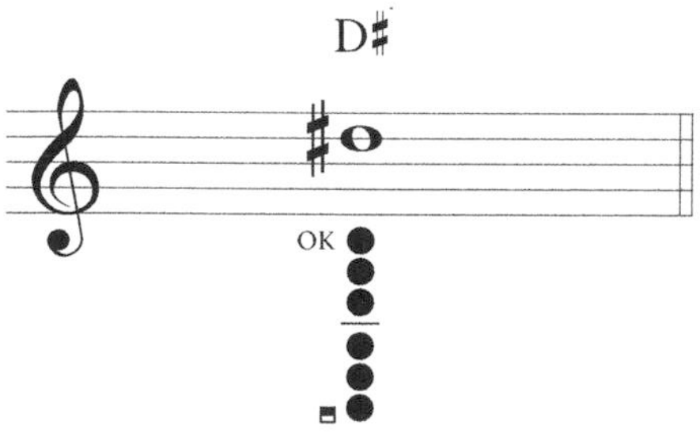

Notice that D♯ sounds the same as E♭. Because of this, they share the same fingering.

Take Me Out to the Ballgame

Albert Von Tilzer

Articulation

Articulation marks give definition to written notes. We use the tongue to make these articulations by stopping the reed from vibrating for an instant.

"Slur two, tongue two" is a common articulation on woodwind instruments. It's also called "tiya tata." A dot under or over a note means play it *staccato,* or very short.

Minuet

J.S. Bach

High Notes

New notes: B, C♯, and D.

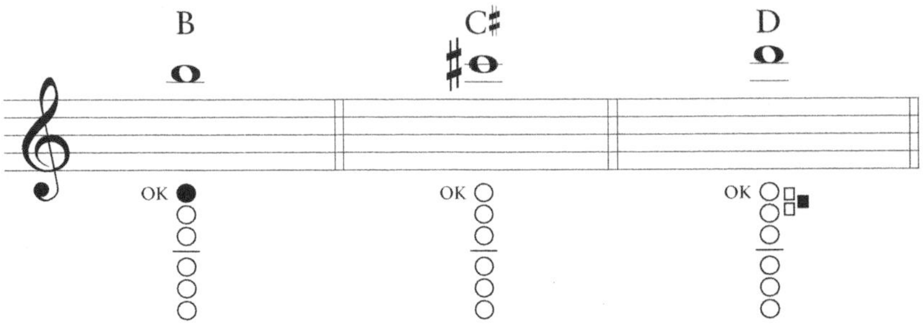

D Major Scale

B Natural Minor Scale

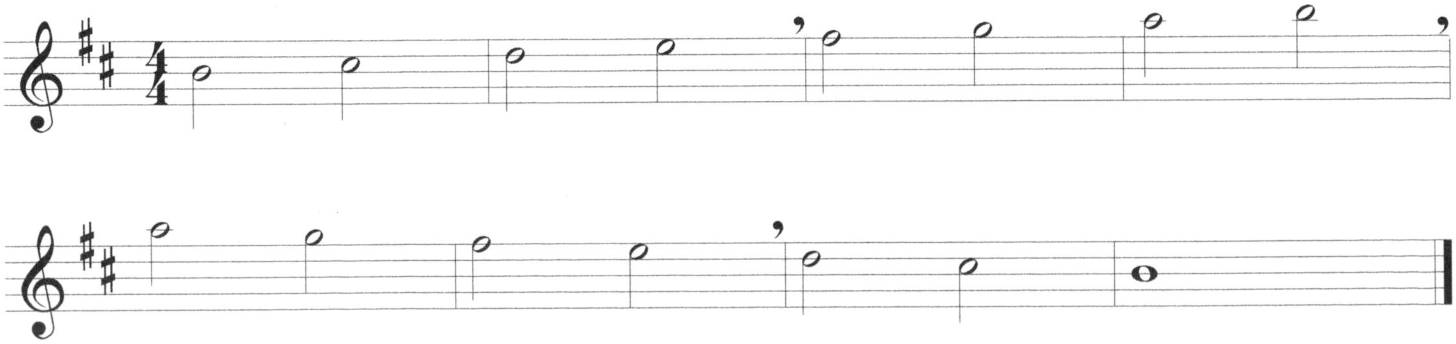

Tum Balalaika

Yiddish

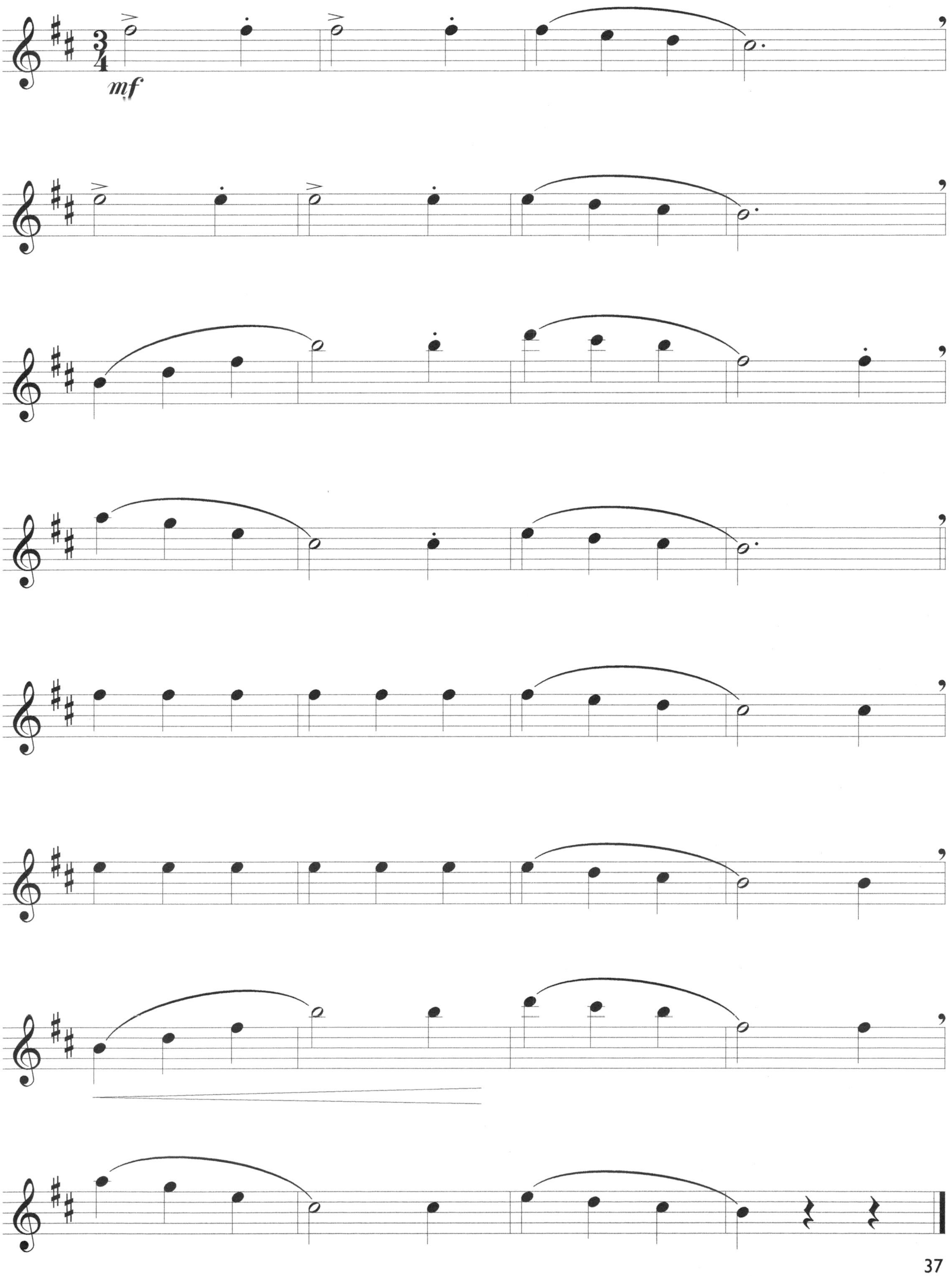

On this next song, play through to the *first ending,* then go back to the beginning and go through the song again, this time skipping the first ending and playing the *second ending* instead.

Watch for the accidentals! A *fermata* (𝄐) means hold the note a little longer. We call it a "bird's eye" for short.

Boogie Woogie

Jazzy Blues

In $\frac{6}{8}$ time, there are six eighth-notes, or the equivalent, in a bar. Since the eighth notes are usually divided into two groups of three, music in $\frac{6}{8}$ time is usually counted "in two." This time signature is found frequently in marches, folk songs, and various types of ethnic music.

When Johnny Comes Marching Home

Traditional

Anchors Aweigh

Navy Song

This Little Light o' Mine

Spiritual

Fingering Chart

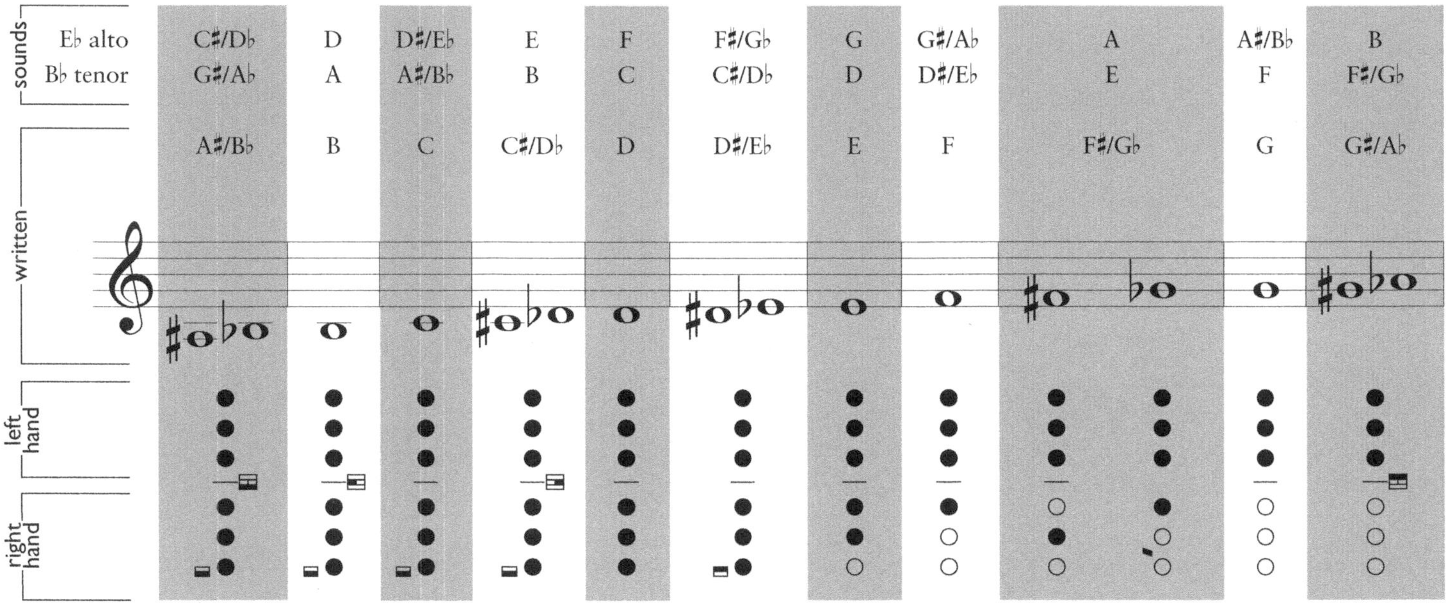

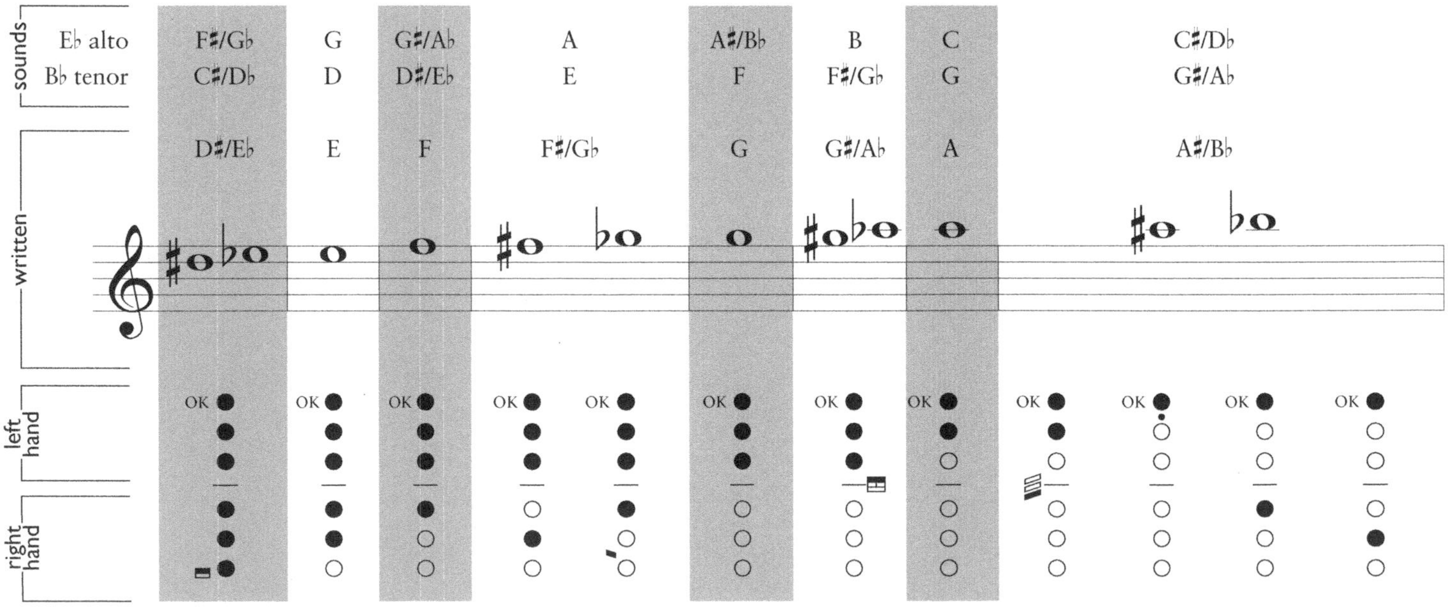

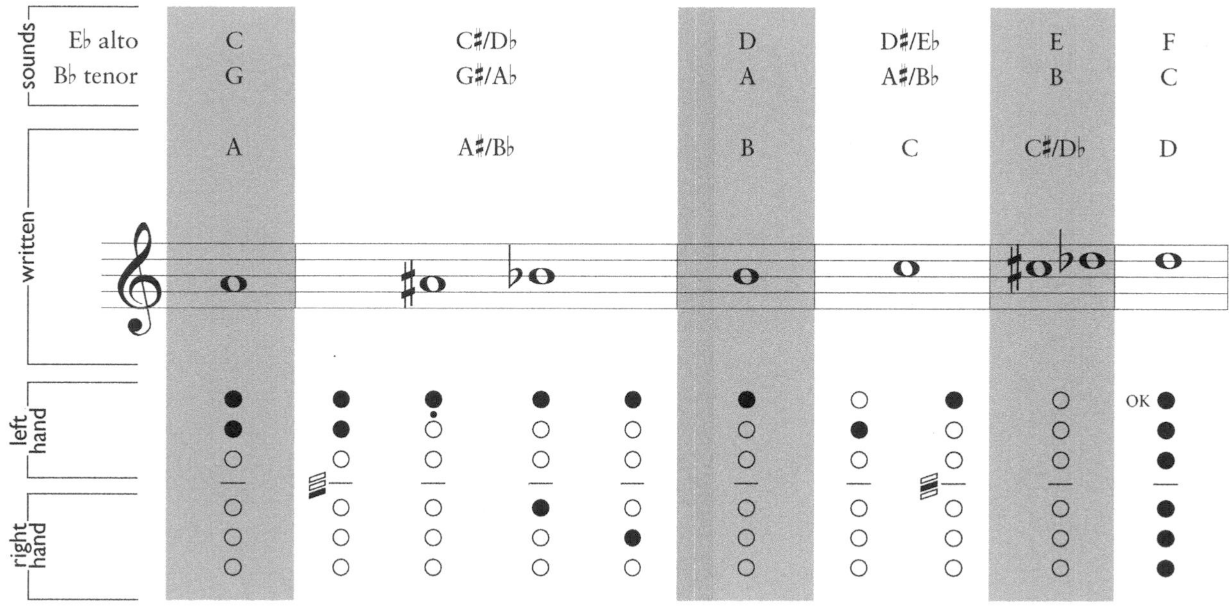
sounds
E♭ alto
B♭ tenor
written
left hand
right hand
C
G
A
C♯/D♭
G♯/A♭
A♯/B♭
D
A
B
D♯/E♭
A♯/B♭
C
E
B
C♯/D♭
F
C
D
OK

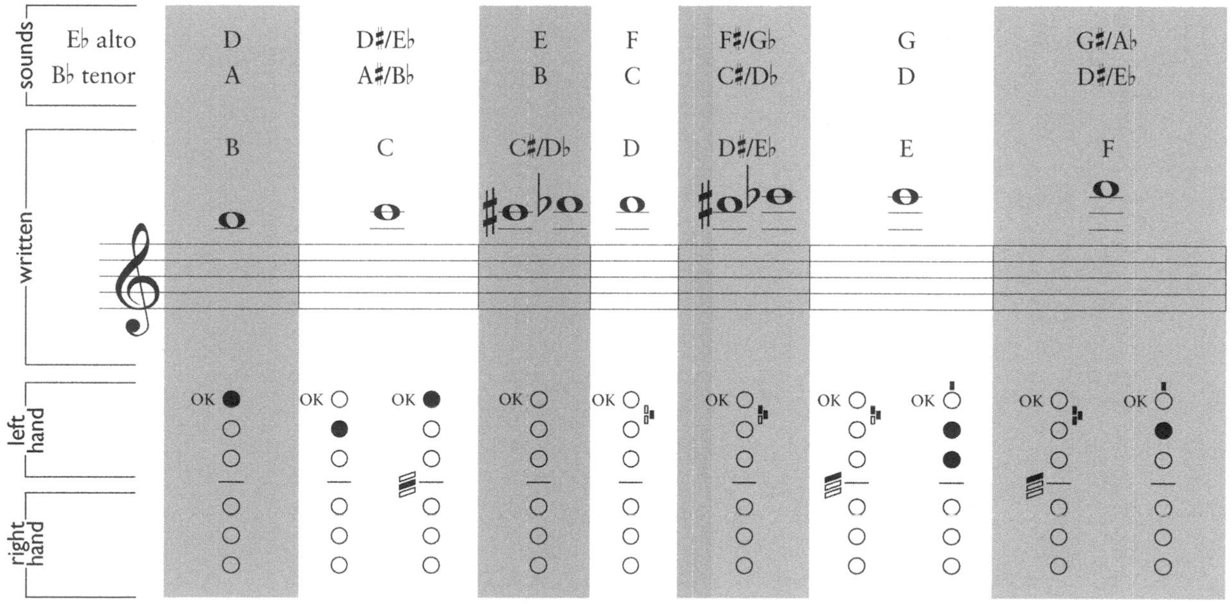
sounds
E♭ alto
B♭ tenor
written
left hand
right hand
D
A
B
D♯/E♭
A♯/B♭
C
E
B
C♯/D♭
F
C
D
F♯/G♭
C♯/D♭
D♯/E♭
G
D
E
G♯/A♭
D♯/E♭
F
OK

Recorded Online Audio

1. Introduction
2. Longtones, First Note: B, and Tuning
3. Whole-Note Exercise
4. Tonguing and New Notes: A and G
5. Half-Note Exercise
6. B, A, and G Exercise
7. *Au Clair de la Lune*
8. *Hot Cross Buns*
9. New Note: C
10. G, A, B, and C Exercise
11. B-to-C Exercise
12. 2/4 Exercise
13. *Bile 'Em Cabbage Down*
14. New Note: F
15. *Mary Had a Little Lamb*
16. *Jazzy Mary*
17. New Note: B♭
18. B♭ Exercise
19. *When the Saints Go Marchin' In*
20. *Lightly Row* (duet)
21. New Note: E
22. New Note: D
23. New Note: C
24. C Major Scale
25. *Getting Down*
26. *Joy to the World*
27. *The Streets of Laredo*
28. New Note: F
29. Octave Exercise 1
30. New Note: E
31. New Note: D
32. Octave Exercise 2
33. F Major Scale
34. *On Top of Old Smokey*
35. *Frère Jacques*
36. C-to-D Exercise
37. New Note: F♯
38. G Major Scale
39. *Auld Lang Syne*
40. *My Country 'Tis of Thee*
41. New Note: C♯
42. *America the Beautiful*
43. New Note: E♭
44. New Note: A
45. New Note: B♭
46. B♭ Major Scale
47. *The John B. Sails*
48. New Note: A♭
49. *De Colores*
50. New Note: D♯
51. *Take Me Out to the Ballgame*
52. *Minuet*
53. New Note: B
54. New Note: C♯
55. New Note: D
56. D Major Scale
57. B Natural Minor Scale
58. *Tum Balalaika*
59. *Boogie Woogie*
60. *Jazzy Blues*
61. *When Johnny Comes Marching Home*
62. *Anchors Aweigh*
63. *This Little Light of Mine*
64. Afterword

Afterword

The best way to go further with your saxophone skills is to study privately with a good teacher. Saxophone teachers can be found in your neighborhood, your local music store, and among the faculty *and students* at your local college. It's also essential to listen to your instrument being played by a professional. Listen to live concerts and recordings of saxophone music. There are many amazing saxophonists on recordings and performing live; here are just a few:

Some notable classical saxophone recordings

Tim McAllister/Duo Nuova *Visions* (Centaur)
Jean-Marie Londeix/Marcel Mule/Daniel Deffayet Quartet compilation *Le Saxophone Français* (EMI)
John-Edward Kelly *Saxophone Concertos* (Arte Nova)
Prism Quartet *The Prism Quartet* (Koch Classical)
Arno Bornkamp *Saxophone Sonatas* (Globe)

Some notable jazz saxophonists

Pepper Adams
Gary Bartz
Sidney Bechet
Jane Ira Bloom
Arthur Blythe
Don Braden
Carol Chaikin
John Coltrane
Junior Cook
Sheila Cooper
Eric Dolphy
Lou Donaldson
Laura Dreyer
Stan Getz
David Glasser
Dexter Gordon
Coleman Hawkins
Jenny Hill
Clifford Jordan
Lee Konitz
Virginia Mayhew
Jackie McLean
Rene McLean
Charles McPherson
Charlie Parker
Sonny Rollins
Dave Sanborn
Wayne Shorter
Sonny Stitt
Grover Washington
Ben Webster
Phil Woods
Lester Young

As your skills improve and you get more and more accustomed to playing your instrument, try out some other mouthpieces and ligatures, to see if they are more comfortable than what you're currently using.

Play by yourself, seek out other people to play with, and play along with your favorite recordings. Above all, have fun!

About the Author

Sue Terry began her professional career in Hartford, Connecticut, where she was a graduate of the Hartt School, and a protégé of saxophonist Jackie McLean. She also studied saxophone with Robert Kolb and Paul Jeffrey; composition with Edward Diemente; jazz with Jaki Byard, Walter Bishop, Jr., and Alexander Lepak; piano and theory with John Mehegan; and the Kodaly System with Janos Horvath, Gabriella Thesz, Maria Farkas, and Tibor Szabo. She settled in New York in 1982, where her mentors—Barry Harris, Clifford Jordan, and Junior Cook—dubbed her "Sweet Sue."

Ms. Terry has worked with Dr. Billy Taylor, Clark Terry, Al Jarreau, Walter Bishop, Jr., Chaka Khan, George Duke, Hilton Ruiz, Irene Reid, Juan Carlos Formell, Dr. John, Teri Thornton, Mike Longo, and Dianne Reeves, among others. She has appeared as a soloist with the National Symphony, the Brooklyn Philharmonic, the Downtown Chamber Players, and the New York Pops conducted by Skitch Henderson. She has performed in many Broadway and Off-Broadway orchestras, including *Cabaret* and *Bring In Da Noise, Bring In Da Funk.*

Her compositions are featured on *The Troubadours* (Consolidated Artists) as co-leader of Terra Mars. Other artists whose recordings have featured her playing and writing include Charli Persip, Clifford Jordan, Joe McMahon, Jazzberry Jam, Derwyn Holder, Mini All Stars, Jaki Byard, Ricardo Franck, Fred Ho, and DIVA. She is Musical Director of the dance/music ensemble Beauteez 'n the Beat.

Widely known as an educator, she has conducted numerous clinics, workshops and lectures throughout the U.S. A longtime practitioner of the ancient arts of *Taiji* and *Qigong,* she is a certified teacher of the Six Healing Sounds.

More about Ms. Terry can be found at www.sueterry.net.

Sue Terry is a Yamaha artist.

Other books by Sue Terry:
Practice like the Pros: Saxophone
Step One: Play Clarinet